DOMINOES

Romeo and Juliet 2079

Founder Editors: Bill Bowler and Sue Parminter

Series Editor: Nicole Irving

Text adaptation by Andrew Prentice

Illustrated by Neil Evans

Andrew Prentice lives in London with his wife, three daughters, and his dog. He feels lucky every day because he can write stories for his job and take his dog for long walks. He also enjoys pretending to be a wizard and imagining ways to end the world.

OXFORD
UNIVERSITY PRESS

OXFORD
UNIVERSITY PRESS

Great Clarendon Street, Oxford, OX2 6DP, United Kingdom

Oxford University Press is a department of the University of Oxford.
It furthers the University's objective of excellence in research, scholarship,
and education by publishing worldwide. Oxford is a registered trade
mark of Oxford University Press in the UK and in certain other countries

This edition © Oxford University Press 2018

The moral rights of the author have been asserted

First published in Dominoes 2018
2024
10 9 8 7

No unauthorized photocopying

ISBN: 978 0 19 460772 8   Book
ISBN: 978 0 19 460771 1   Book and Audio Pack

Audio not available separately

Printed in China

This book is printed on paper from certified and well-managed sources

ACKNOWLEDGEMENTS

Cover illustrations by: Neil Evans/The Bright Agency

Illustrations by: Neil Evans/The Bright Agency

The publisher would like to thank the following for permission to reproduce photographs:
Shutterstock p.49 (The Colosseum, Rome/Alexandr Medvedkov).

Contents

BEFORE READING

1 **Here are some of the people in *Romeo and Juliet 2079*. Match each sentence with a picture. Use a dictionary to help you.**

1 Romeo

2 Juliet

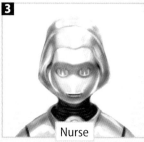
3 Nurse

4 Tybalt

5 Mercutio

6 The gene-fixer

a ☐ A brave young mechanic, who wants to escape; he's a Normal.

b ☐ A rich young woman; she's a Perfect.

c ☐ A dying man, Romeo's brother.

d ☐ An angry Perfect, Juliet's brother, who hates Normals.

e ☐ A teacher and Juliet's guard; she's a robot.

f ☐ A doctor who can change someone's blood, fingerprints, and eyes.

2 **What do you think happens in the story? Complete the sentences with the names from Activity 1.**

a .... needs to find medicine for ....

b .... will go to school in Rome.

c .... carries a gun and drives a fast car.

d .... makes someone look different.

e .... helps Romeo and Juliet.

Compare your ideas with a partner.

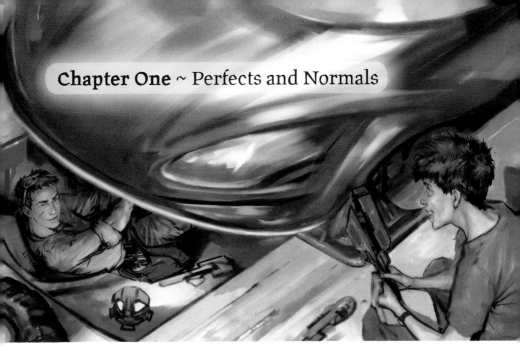

Chapter One ~ Perfects and Normals

'You know what, Romeo?' said Mercutio. 'I like red cars.'

'That's nice, little brother,' said Romeo.

'Yes! One day I'll buy a red car. No, I'll buy two! And then I'll drive around Verona and all the girls will love me.'

Mercutio **coughed** hard.

'Are you OK?' asked Romeo.

'Pah! I'm as strong as a horse. All the girls know that, too. Do you think that they'll like my red car, Romeo?'

Romeo looked up from his work. He was lying under the red car in a dirty hole, working on the wheels. His dark hair was dirty. His clothes and face were even dirtier. He knew that he smelled bad.

'Stop **dreaming** – and forget the red car, Mercutio,' said Romeo, smiling. 'You never do any work!'

Mercutio laughed. It was true; he liked talking – and dreaming – much more than working. His clothes were never dirty. 'That's why I enjoy watching you down there.'

'If you won't help, make me some tea,' said Romeo.

'All right, brother.' Mercutio went to the kitchen. Romeo heard his cough – and he was afraid.

cough when you make a noise in your throat because you are ill; to make a noise in your throat

dream something that you see pictures in your head when you are sleeping

Romeo had no money because there were no cars to mend. **Normals** did not drive cars. The brothers usually mended other **broken** things. There was a little work with that, because everything was old and broken in Verona.

Only **Perfects** had money for cars, and not many Perfects ever came to Verona. Perfects lived in New Town, behind high walls. Perfects liked everything to be modern and tidy.

When the brothers were young, their father told them stories: in the old times, he said, everyone was born the same – they weren't Normal or Perfect; everyone went to school and had money and a car; everyone lived for seventy years or more.

Life was good then.

But Romeo's father and mother both died from The Coughing **Plague** years ago. They died very young. 'All Normals die young now,' Romeo thought. 'If I have good luck, I'll possibly live to be thirty years old.'

His brother Mercutio always had bad luck. He was only seventeen, and already he had a cough.

Perfects did not cough. They did not die young. Some of them never died. It was not right, but that was how it was now.

For a minute or two, while Romeo pushed and pulled at the broken wheel, he forgot all his troubles. He did not remember that he had no money or that his brother was unwell. He was happy.

Romeo liked mending things, and he loved mending beautiful things like this red car. He was clever with his hands, and he was much cleverer than the stupid boy who crashed it.

That stupid boy was a Perfect called Tybalt. 'How did Tybalt crash his car into a tree?' thought Romeo. 'Well, it's work for me.'

Tybalt did not want his father to know about his accident, so he asked the brothers to mend the car.

Ten minutes later, Romeo finished pushing the wheel into place. 'I'm nearly done,' he shouted. 'Where's that tea?'

'Coming,' said Mercutio. He coughed again. 'Uh-oh! And here comes Tybalt, too.'

workshop a room where you do work with your hands

Two boys walked into the **workshop**. They were both tall and wore expensive clothes. Their hair was beautiful and their teeth were very white.

Romeo climbed out from under the car. He smiled. Tybalt did not smile back.

'It smells like poor people here,' said Tybalt.

His friend laughed.

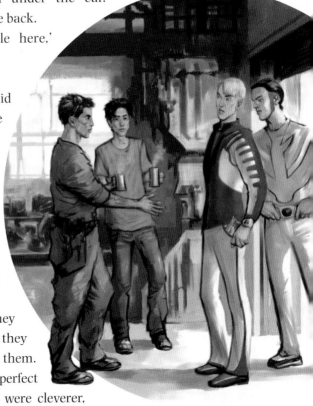

'Ha-ha! Thank you,' said Mercutio. 'We do our best.' He walked into the workshop, carrying two cups of tea.

The two boys looked at him coldly. But Romeo was looking at them: it was always interesting to see Perfects. These boys were not very different to him, Romeo could see.

Perfects all thought that they were better because before they were born, doctors changed them. The doctors made each baby perfect inside their mother. So they were cleverer, and more beautiful, and always much richer. They were not always nicer.

'And they still eat and drink and sleep like me,' thought Romeo.

He went to shake Tybalt's hand.

Tybalt did not take it.

'You're dirty,' he said. 'Have you touched my car?'

'I was mending it,' said Romeo. 'So I did touch it, yes.'

fool someone who cannot think well

throw (*past* **threw**) to make something move from your hand through the air

'Urgh!' Tybalt replied, coldly again. 'Give me the keys! I want to get away from here.'

'That's interesting,' said Mercutio in a friendly voice.

'What's interesting?'

'You're more stupid than I thought.'

'What did you say?' said Tybalt. He looked angry.

'I said that you're very stupid,' said Mercutio.

'Careful, brother.' Romeo was not afraid, but he knew that these boys were dangerous.

But Mercutio was never careful.

'I mean, who crashes into a tree?' he said. 'A stupid **fool** who–'

Tybalt jumped on Mercutio. He tried to hit him, but Mercutio was too quick. He took one of the cups from the table and then he **threw** hot tea in Tybalt's face – and in his eyes.

'It burns!' screamed Tybalt.

Mercutio caught Tybalt and tried to shake him. Just then, something fell from Tybalt's pocket.

Now Tybalt's friend, Sampson, pulled out a gun.

'Woah! Easy,' said Romeo. He pushed his brother away. 'It's all OK.'

'It's not OK!' shouted Tybalt. 'Shoot them!'

But his friend looked worried. He moved the gun from Romeo to Mercutio. Now Mercutio was quiet.

'I don't want trouble,' said Sampson.

'That's all right,' said Romeo. 'I don't want trouble either.'

Romeo stood very still, but Mercutio began to cough hard.

'Oh no! That one's unwell,' said Tybalt's friend. 'See, he has a cough. We need to leave now.'

'I can't see anything!' shouted Tybalt. He still had his hands over his eyes.

Sampson helped Tybalt into the car, and they drove away fast.

'Stupid! Rich! Lazy!' shouted Mercutio, and then he had to cough again.

'Oh brother, they didn't pay us,' said Romeo.

'Stupid rich boys!' said Mercutio.

'But how am I going to pay for things that can help your cough?' asked Romeo.

'Don't worry about it. Wait! What's this?' Mercutio saw some papers on the ground. He held them up in the light.

'It's two **invitations**,' he said. 'Wow! They're invitations to a party in New Town. It's tonight! You have to wear **masks**. Ha-ha! Well! Do you know what we're going to do now?'

'No,' said Romeo. 'No, Mercutio!'

'Yes, brother.' Mercutio coughed again. 'Yes. We'll go to this party.'

'But there'll be guards with guns. It's dangerous.'

'So?' Mercutio shook the invitations at Romeo. 'We'll walk past them with these. It'll be easy.'

'We'll die,' said Romeo.

'No. Listen to me,' said Mercutio. 'You know that I'll never have a red car, brother.' He coughed hard again.

'Don't say that, Mercutio.'

'No. Listen to my cough, brother. You know that I'll never see another winter.'

'But–'

'That's right. We'll wear masks and we'll go to this party,' Mercutio said, and he smiled.

invitation a letter asking you to go somewhere

mask something that you wear over your face to hide it

5

ACTIVITIES

READING CHECK

Are these sentences true or false? Tick (✔) the boxes.

		True	False
a	Romeo and Mercutio are sisters.	☐	☑
b	Verona is a happy place.	☐	☐
c	Romeo is poor.	☐	☐
d	Tybalt crashed his car into a house.	☐	☐
e	Normals drive cars.	☐	☐
f	Perfects do not get ill.	☐	☐
g	Mercutio doesn't like Tybalt.	☐	☐
h	Romeo wants to go to the party.	☐	☐

WORD WORK

1 Find six more words from Chapter 1 in the letter square.

broken   ~~cough~~   dream   fool   invitation   mask   normal   perfect   plague   workshop

6

ACTIVITIES

2 Complete the sentences with the correct form of the words in Activity 1.

a The smoke from the fire gave me a ..... cough ..... .

b My .... is to go to Disneyland Paris one day.

c What time is it? My watch is ....

d In the story, ... don't have any money.

e .... are very rich in the story, and like everything to be modern and tidy.

f Do you have your .... to the party? You won't get in without it!

g No one saw the thief's face because he was wearing a ....

h Mercutio thinks Tybalt is a stupid ....

i The .... was full of broken cars and old wheels.

j Romeo's father and mother both died from the Coughing ....

GUESS WHAT

What happens in the next chapter? Tick (✔) three boxes.

a ☐ Mercutio dies.

b ☐ Romeo goes to the party.

c ☐ Romeo loses the invitation.

d ☐ Tybalt tries to kill Romeo.

e ☐ Tybalt and Mercutio make friends.

f ☐ Mercutio falls in love with a girl.

g ☐ Romeo falls in love with a girl.

Chapter Two ~ Meeting Juliet

Mercutio worried while he and Romeo waited to get into the party. Everyone there was a Perfect. They wore expensive clothes and clever masks. Romeo and Mercutio had paper masks. Romeo's mask was a dog and Mercutio's was a fish.

'If they catch us, brother, they'll kill us,' said Romeo. 'Why are we here?' He was **shivering**.

'Be quiet,' said Mercutio.

'This was your plan, remember,' said Romeo. 'Where are the invitations?'

'In my pocket.'

'OK. Here we go.' The music from the party was very loud. A woman was singing.

Romeo and Mercutio walked to the door. A **guard** was **scanning** all the invitations. They could see his silver gun. He **frowned** at their clothes.

'So. You're Tybalt and Sampson, yes?' asked the guard.

'That's right. I'm Tybalt and that's Sampson,' said Romeo. He was afraid, but he tried to hide it. His voice shook.

'Hmm.' The guard looked at his scanner, and looked at them again. Romeo wanted to run away, but at last the guard smiled.

'Enjoy the party,' he said.

They walked in. Now they were excited.

'Oh, brother!' said Mercutio. 'We did it! This is the luckiest day of our lives!'

Mercutio was enjoying being there, Romeo could see.

The house looked wonderful. There were flowers everywhere, and **robots** with food and drink. Mercutio took a sandwich and a blue drink in a glass.

'Have a nice evening,' said the robot.

'Hah! I will, friend!' shouted Mercutio.

He ran deep into the crowd and began dancing wildly.

Romeo watched while Mercutio enjoyed the party and talked to beautiful girls in dresses that cost more than a Normal's house. Romeo's head was full of music. 'I'm dreaming!' he thought. Everything smelled of summer. Everyone was beautiful.

It was strange: for Perfect people, all this was very usual.

'But I will never see a place like this again,' thought Romeo. 'And my brother will die while I watch, and I can do nothing to help him.' Suddenly nothing felt good.

Behind him he heard a man shouting.

'I *can* come in!' It was Tybalt. 'Do you *know* who I am?'

'If you don't have an invitation,' said the guard at the door, 'you can't come in.'

'You dog!' Tybalt cried. 'I am Tybalt Capulet! And I'm going to *my* party!' He tried to push past the guard.

Now Romeo was worried again – he did not want Tybalt to see him. He looked for Mercutio, but he could not see his brother in the crowd. Romeo walked quickly away from the house and into the garden. It was quiet there. The trees were old and tall.

He sat near some beautiful flowers. He looked around. Was he alone? The garden was empty. He took off his mask. He felt tired.

'Don't you like the party?' said a voice. A girl's voice.

Romeo jumped and dropped the mask. The girl laughed.

robot a machine that looks and moves like a person or animal

9

'Where are you?' asked Romeo.

'Up here,' said the voice.

A girl was sitting in the tree above Romeo's head. She was not wearing a mask. She had a book and a red apple. She smiled down at him, and with that one smile, Romeo **fell in love**.

'My family spends all their money on these terrible people. It's stupid', she said. 'That's why I'm hiding up here.'

'This is *your* house – is that what you mean?' said Romeo. He wanted to hide behind his mask, but he could not stop looking at the girl. Her face was beautiful. Her eyes...

'Yes.' She smiled again. 'My name's Juliet. And you are... ?'

'Romeo.'

'I don't think that I've seen you before, Romeo.' She frowned.

'I'm... I'm not from around here.'

Juliet jumped from the tree. She looked carefully at Romeo – and his **heart** jumped. She was better than perfect.

'No,' she said. 'You're not.' Her eyes were slowly going over his clothes and his face.

Suddenly, Romeo was afraid. Perhaps she knew his secret. But he could not turn away.

He was **staring** into her eyes, and their faces nearly touched.

'Don't worry, Romeo,' she said. 'I won't tell anyone.'

'Romeo! Romeo!' It was Mercutio. He was **running** through the garden. 'Run! Tybalt saw me. He wants to kill us!'

Juliet's face changed.

'Go!' she told Romeo. 'I'll send my brother the wrong way. There's a **gate** in the wall at the bottom of the garden. It's open.'

'Thank you!' said Romeo. He did not want to leave her, but he knew that if Tybalt found him here, he was in danger.

Juliet took his hand.

'Please come back and see me,' she said. 'Later. At the gate in the wall. **Promise**.'

'I promise.'

'Leave her, Romeo!' said Mercutio. 'Tybalt's got a gun, you must leave NOW!'

They went quietly through the gate. Half a minute later, they heard Tybalt – he was shouting, and then Juliet told him that two men were running to the top of the garden.

'You're smiling, brother,' said Mercutio. 'Romeo! You never smile. What's happened to you?'

'Juliet,' Romeo replied.

stare to look at someone or something for a long time

gate a door in a garden or in a town wall

promise to say now that you will do something later

READING CHECK

Put these sentences in the correct order. Number them 1–8.

a ☐ Mercutio started dancing.

b ☐ Romeo and Mercutio walked into the party.

c ☐ Juliet took Romeo's hand. She asked Romeo to come back and see her.

d ☐ Romeo sat down in the quiet garden.

e ☐ The guard scanned the invitation and frowned.

f ☐ Juliet jumped from the tree.

g ☐ Tybalt saw Mercutio. Mercutio ran through the garden to tell Romeo.

h ☐ Romeo fell in love with Juliet.

WORD WORK

1 Use the clues to complete the crossword on page 13 with new words from Chapter 2.

Down

a To look at somebody or something for a long time.

b To read information with a machine.

f This sends blood around your body.

g This looks and moves like a person, but isn't.

Across

c To say that you will do something.

d Your face does this when you are angry or worried.

e To shake because you're afraid or cold.

h A big door into a garden.

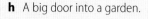

2 Use words from Chapter 2 to correct the boxed words in these sentences.

scanner

a The officer used a `scan` to read the passport.

b Will you `robot` to be on time?

c The `heart` stopped people from going into the museum.

d I think I am `shivering` in love with you!

e Romeo's `frown` jumped when he looked at Juliet.

GUESS WHAT

What does Juliet do in the next chapter? Tick (✔) three boxes.

Juliet

She ...

a ☐ forgets about Romeo.

b ☐ falls in love with Romeo.

c ☐ talks to Mercutio.

d ☐ visits Verona.

e ☐ goes away to school.

f ☐ fights with her mother and father.

13

Chapter Three ~ Together?

Juliet was waiting at the gate when Romeo arrived. It was already past midnight.

'You came back!' she said. 'I thought that you wouldn't.'

She was smiling. Romeo's heart jumped again.

'Tybalt's very angry because of you,' she said.

'I'm sorry.'

'Don't be! My brother is a rich fool.'

'He is, yes.'

Juliet's laugh was like sweet music. 'But tell me: what are *you*, Romeo?'

Romeo was ready for this. He wanted to tell her the **truth**.

'I'm a Normal. I live in Verona and **fix** cars and other things.'

'Good,' said Juliet. 'I knew when I saw you without your mask that you were not like me.'

She moved nearer to him. Her hand touched his hand.

'You're so alive,' she said. '*I'm* not.'

'Juliet!' said a strange, flat voice behind her. 'That is not true. You *are* alive, you are not dead.'

Romeo jumped.

'Don't worry!' said Juliet. 'That's just Nurse. She's always with me, and we're friends.'

'She's a robot?' asked Romeo.

'I am Juliet's robot,' said Nurse. 'I am her teacher and her guard. My job is to keep her alive. And you *are* alive, Juliet.'

'It's OK, Nurse,' said Juliet. 'Please watch the garden. Tell me if someone comes.'

'You have a robot?' said Romeo.

truth what is true

fix to make OK again, to mend

kiss to touch lovingly with your lips; a loving touch with the lips

'Be quiet,' said Juliet and she **kissed** him.

Romeo and Juliet met secretly every day for a month. It was the happiest month of their lives. Sometimes they met in Juliet's garden. They spent nights sitting near the sweet-smelling flowers, talking about everything. Nurse guarded them and

city (*plural* **cities**)
a big and
important town

listened to their stories. They only stopped talking when the sky turned red and the last silver star was gone.

They had to be very careful. 'If anyone sees you, they'll kill you,' Juliet told Romeo. It was dangerous, so every minute together was even sweeter.

Juliet was a Perfect and Romeo was a Normal, but they were not so different, they soon found out. They liked the same things and were deeply in love.

Sometimes Juliet went into Verona. Here, too, they had to be careful. In the Normals' **city**, Juliet had to hide her face.

Romeo showed her his life. They went to a football **game** and ate hamburgers. He taught her how to fix a car. One evening, they sat near the river and gave food to the wild cats. Juliet liked Mercutio, too. She thought that he was funny, and when she came to the workshop she always laughed and laughed. She brought him **medicine** for his cough, and fruit.

Everything was going well. But a dark cloud was coming.

Juliet was leaving soon. All Perfects had to go to a special school when they were eighteen. The school was in the city of Rome. Normals could not go into Rome because the city was afraid of The Coughing Plague. The walls around it were high.

'If I go inside the walls,' said Juliet, 'you won't see me for years.'

She and Romeo began to make plans to run away.

But Romeo worried. 'If you stay here with us Normals, you'll get ill.' There was no medicine in Verona. Juliet did not listen. She wanted to stay with Romeo.

People said that in Paris, Normals and Perfects lived together freely and happily. Paris was far away, and there were many dangers on the road to Paris, but Romeo and Juliet decided to run away there together. They wanted to take Mercutio, too, and try to keep him alive.

game something that you play

medicine something that you eat or drink to help you get better when you are ill

'Don't take me with you,' said Mercutio. 'You'll be slower with me.'

'Don't be stupid. I won't leave you, brother,' said Romeo.

'You two love birds need me like a bicycle needs a third wheel,' said Mercutio.

'I think that you'll like Paris,' Juliet told him. 'People say that there are really good hospitals there, too.'

'I don't know,' said Mercutio. 'How much do you like cold winters? I like our Verona sun better. I'm staying.'

But they did not listen. 'I won't go without you,' said Romeo.

It was exciting to make secret plans. Juliet sold some things in the market to get more money. Romeo bought a gun, too, because there were dangerous people in the mountains and thieves on the roads. They both began to hope.

On the last night before they left, they met one more time in Juliet's garden. They talked about the next day. Romeo said goodbye to Nurse. The robot was his friend now. Nurse was staying at the house to send anyone who looked for them the wrong way.

Romeo said goodbye to Juliet with a kiss.

'I will see you tomorrow, my love,' she said.

Romeo went to the garden gate and opened it. He stopped just before he went through, and turned back. He wanted to give Juliet one more kiss.

It was a terrible mistake.

'Hey!'

Suddenly Romeo was standing in a bright light.

'What are you doing here?' Tybalt was in the garden!

'I will kill you, Romeo,' shouted Tybalt.

Romeo could not see anything. The light was too bright. He started to move away.

'Run!' screamed Juliet.

Romeo turned and ran. Tybalt moved his gun up.

BANG! BANG! BANG!

One **bullet** hit a tree, another hit the wall, and the third bullet hit the gate just above Romeo's head.

bullet a small piece of metal that you shoot from a gun

Behind him, Romeo heard Tybalt's shouts.

READING CHECK

Match the first and second parts of the sentences.

a Nurse …

b Juliet was waiting at the gate …

c Mercutio was funny …

d Juliet had to go to a special school when …

e Juliet and Romeo …

f Romeo taught Juliet …

g Tybalt saw …

h Perfects and Normals lived together freely …

1 made secret plans together.

2 how to fix a car.

3 when Romeo arrived.

4 she was eighteen.

5 and Juliet liked him.

6 Romeo and Juliet together.

7 is Juliet's teacher and guard.

8 in Paris.

WORD WORK

1 Find new words from Chapter 3 in the flowers.

a c i t y

b _ _ _ _

c _ _ _ _ _ _

d _ _ _ _ _

e _ _ _ _ _

f _ _ _ _

g _ _ _ _ _ _ _ _

2 Complete the sentences with the words in the correct form from Activity 1.

a Madrid is a .... c.i.t.y ...... in Spain.

b Helen was bad, because she didn't tell the ....

c A .... from a gun can kill you.

d Ann could .... broken computers.

e My mother .... me goodbye.

f Barcelona won the football .... against Valencia.

g .... can make you better.

GUESS WHAT

What do you think happens in the next chapter? Tick (✔) three boxes.

a ☐ Tybalt kills Mercutio.

b ☐ Mercutio laughs at Romeo.

c ☐ Romeo kills Tybalt.

d ☐ Juliet goes to Rome.

e ☐ Juliet kills Tybalt.

f ☐ Mercutio dies.

Chapter Four ~ Tybalt is angry

Romeo ran home as fast as he could. He wanted to tell Mercutio to hide – Tybalt was coming.

But when he arrived at his workshop, he saw Tybalt's car outside. Its lights were on. The workshop door was open. He heard shouts and crashes. He ran in.

Mercutio was running around the room. He was trying to stay away from Tybalt. Tybalt's face was red and angry. His eyes were wild, and he looked like a **mad** animal.

'Where's your brother?' shouted Tybalt. 'I'm going to kill him!'

'Hmm,' said Mercutio. 'Perhaps he's kissing your sister?'

Tybalt screamed again and tried to catch Mercutio. But Mercutio was ready and jumped away.

'Stay still,' said Tybalt. 'You **filthy** Normal.'

'Stop,' said Romeo. 'Here I am.'

Tybalt turned around, and his hand went to his pocket.

'Let's talk about this,' said Romeo.

'If you hurt my family, there will be trouble!' said Tybalt.

'I didn't hurt anyone,' said Romeo.

'Ask Juliet,' said Mercutio. 'She's not hurt – she's very happy!'

'Shut up,' said Tybalt softly.

'You can't tell me what to do,' said Mercutio.

'*This* can,' Tybalt replied. He pulled out his gun and **pointed** it at Romeo. 'Tell your brother to be quiet.'

'It's OK, Mercutio,' said Romeo. 'What do you want, Tybalt?'

'I want your life. I want blood.'

'Juliet is–' Romeo started to say.

'Don't say her name,' shouted Tybalt. 'No filthy Normal talks about my sister!'

'Why?' shouted Romeo. He knew that it was better to be **calm**, but he could not stop himself. 'She loves me. I love her.'

'You cannot!' screamed Tybalt. He was shaking and crying. 'My sister doesn't love a filthy Normal!'

mad not thinking well, crazy

filthy very dirty

point to show something with a stick or a finger

calm not worried; not moving very fast

Romeo was watching the end of the gun very carefully. He was looking at it very hard, so when Mercutio slowly moved nearer to Tybalt, he did not see him. And he did not see the bottle in Mercutio's hand.

'Why don't you put the gun down?' said Romeo.

'No! No,' said Tybalt. 'Get on the floor!'

Tybalt was not watching Mercutio. So he was surprised when Mercutio hit him on the head with the bottle.

Tybalt fell to the floor and dropped his gun.

'Ha-ha!' said Mercutio. 'You aren't so strong now, are you?'

He moved his arm to hit Tybalt with the bottle again. It was a big, heavy green bottle. Romeo saw blood in Tybalt's hair.

'Don't hit him again,' said Romeo. 'You'll kill him.'

Mercutio looked unsure. 'But he wants to kill *you*!'

'He's Juliet's brother,' said Romeo. 'So he's our brother, too.'

'I am *not* your brother!' Tybalt screamed. His hand moved fast and he took the gun from the floor.

Mercutio was too slow.

The sound of the gun in the room was very loud.

Mercutio dropped to the floor, holding his stomach. There was blood everywhere.

Romeo was shaking.

'Brother!' he shouted. And angrily, he ran at Tybalt.

Tybalt pointed the gun at Romeo. His finger pulled the **trigger**.

'I'm going to die,' thought Romeo. Time was moving very slowly. He could see his brother lying on the floor. There was so much blood. He could see the gun and the black hole at the end of it.

trigger you pull this part of a gun to shoot it

click a small noise that a machine makes

He waited for the bullet.

He was surprised when it didn't come.

Click. Click. Tybalt pulled the trigger again, and again. Tybalt was surprised, too. There were no more bullets. His gun was empty. Romeo was very near him now. He saw Tybalt's eyes go dark and afraid.

Then Tybalt was crashing into him. The two boys fell together. Tybalt hit Romeo on the head with the gun, and for a second or two, everything went black.

Romeo's head felt terrible, he was angry, he did not know what he was doing.

His hand found the bottle. He hit Tybalt hard, and then again, a second time.

Tybalt fell down. Blood came from his mouth. His eyes were open, but they did not move. He was dead.

Romeo looked at the bottle in his hand and dropped it.

'Good job, brother,' said Mercutio. 'Now you need to run.'

Romeo went down on the ground beside his brother and took Mercutio's hand. Mercutio's face was very white.

'I'm not leaving you,' Romeo said.

'Leave me!' Mercutio cried. 'You just killed a Perfect. They'll **hunt** everywhere for you. You have to leave Verona – now!'

'I'm not leaving you.'

'I'm dead, brother. Look.' Mercutio moved his hand to show his bloody stomach.

'But...' Romeo put his hand under Mercutio's head. 'You can't die,' he said.

'Why did you stop me? I wanted to kill him.' Mercutio's voice was quiet now.

Romeo could not speak – he was crying.

'I love you, Romeo. You stay alive for me.'

'I'm sorry, brother,' said Romeo. 'Please don't go.'

'A plague on all of it,' said Mercutio.

He closed his eyes.

Mercutio did not **breathe** again.

hunt to look for and kill animals or to look for a person in this way

breathe when you move air into or out of your body

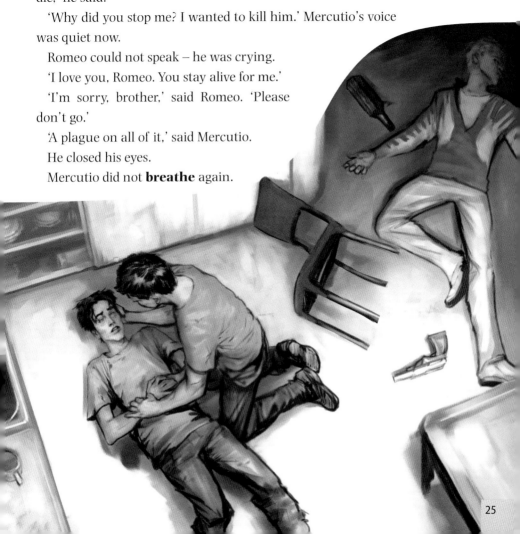

READING CHECK

Correct the mistakes in these sentences.

a Romeo ran home as ~~slowly~~ *fast* as he could.

b When Romeo arrived at the workshop, he saw Juliet's car outside.

c Tybalt pulled a scanner from his pocket.

d Mercutio hit Tybalt with a book.

e The bottle was green and not very heavy.

f The sound of Tybalt's gun was very quiet.

g Mercutio dropped to the floor, holding his arm.

h There were lots of bullets in Tybalt's gun.

i Romeo hit Tybalt hard with the gun.

j Tybalt's eyes were closed but he was alive.

k Romeo killed a Perfect so he must stay in Verona now.

l Mercutio closed his eyes and he was breathing.

WORD WORK

Use the words in the picture of Romeo to complete what he is thinking on page 27.

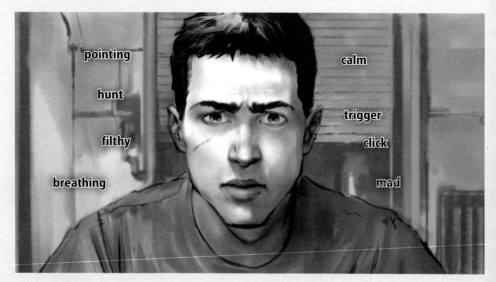

pointing calm hunt trigger filthy click breathing mad

Tybalt is **a)** ..... mad .... He looks like a wild animal!

Tybalt is very angry. He called Mercutio a ' **b)** .... Normal'.

I must not shout. I must stay **c)** ....

I feel afraid. Tybalt is **d)** .... the gun at me.

Why is Tybalt pulling the **e)** .... of the gun again and again? Why am I not dead?

Perhaps if the gun goes **f)** .... , it is empty. There are no more bullets.

My brother has stopped **g)** ....

'I just killed a Perfect. They will **h)** .... everywhere for me. '

GUESS WHAT

What do you think happens in the next chapter? Complete the sentences with the names in the box.

| Romeo Juliet Mercutio Nurse Tybalt |

a The police hunt for .... with dogs and robots.

b .... 's mother and father are sad because he is dead.

c Romeo puts .... in a hole in the ground.

d .... is not free to leave her house.

e .... tries to help Juliet.

Chapter Five ~ Milan and Rome

Romeo knew that he did not have much time. He looked through Tybalt's pockets and found his money. There was not very much. Romeo's bag was ready in his room. He took Tybalt's money, and went and got the bag.

He **dug** a **grave** and put his brother's body carefully into it, then he **covered** the hole again. He was crying all the time.

'Goodbye, brother,' he said for the last time.

Then Romeo put Tybalt's body in his red car and drove it to the river. He sat Tybalt behind the wheel of the car, and then he drove nearer the water. At the last second, Romeo jumped out. The car fell into the river – half-in, half-out. 'The police will think that it was an accident – or that's my hope,' Romeo thought.

But he was very afraid. The police had hunting robots and hunting dogs. 'If they think that someone murdered Tybalt, they'll come to get me,' he thought.

Before the sun was up, Romeo ran into the hills. He did not know where he was going. He wanted to talk to Juliet, but it was too dangerous.

dig (*past* **dug**) to make a hole in the ground

grave a hole in the ground for a dead body

cover to put something over a different thing so it is difficult to see

'And I killed her brother... If she finds out, she'll stop loving me,' he thought. But Romeo could not **lie** to her. So he ran.

Juliet was afraid, too. She could not sleep. Was Romeo alive? What happened with Tybalt? She needed to know. She did not have to wait very long. The police soon came to her **parents'** house. She heard her mother screaming. When she went to them, her father was crying too.

'Tybalt's dead!' her father told her.

When she heard the news, Juliet did not cry. She felt happy, which surprised her. If Tybalt was dead, then perhaps Romeo was still alive, she thought. Then she felt **guilty**. Tybalt was bad, but he was her brother.

The police were **suspicious**. They asked Juliet many questions.

'Did you see Tybalt last night?'

'No, I didn't.'

'Why have you visited Verona so many times?'

'I like to see the old city.'

'Do you know anyone there?'

'No, I don't. Of course not. A Perfect never talks to a Normal.'

The questions took a long time, and the police asked her the same questions again and again.

When Juliet heard that the police found Tybalt's car in the river, she was worried. 'Perhaps Romeo killed Tybalt,' she thought.

The police were still suspicious.

Her mother and father were angry. They asked her the same questions. They were suspicious of her answers, too. Tybalt was always their favourite child – and now he was dead. They stopped her leaving the house. Her home was like a prison.

Juliet's heart was broken. She thought of Romeo every day.

lie to say something that is not true; something that is not true

parent a mother or father

guilty doing something wrong

suspicious when you think that someone has done something bad

In one week, Romeo walked all the way to Milan. This was a dangerous city, but Romeo wanted to hide there. The people in Milan were very poor, and The Coughing Plague was everywhere. All the buildings were falling down, but hundreds of thousands of Normals still lived in the city. Every day someone died from The Coughing Plague.

Because Romeo was good at fixing things, he found a job in a factory. All day long, he thought only of Juliet. He dreamed of her at night. His dreams kept him alive.

~ ~

After two weeks in her room, Juliet was free to leave the house again. She went secretly to Romeo's workshop. Inside, the smell was terrible. She found all the blood, and then she saw the bullet hole in the floor. She looked at the blood and the hole, and she thought, 'Yes, I understand what happened.'

Outside, she found a new grave. 'Mercutio's grave,' she thought. Near the grave there were some stones, and underneath them, she found a picture. 'A picture of Romeo with his brother. Romeo put this here,' Juliet thought, and began to cry.

'I'm sorry, Mercutio,' she said. 'My brother did this to you, and I'm sorry.'

Then she remembered Mercutio's laugh. He was always laughing.

Every day for three months Juliet thought: 'Today is the day when Romeo comes back.' But in the end she stopped hoping. 'I know that I'll never love another man, but I cannot stay in Verona any more.'

Her parents were still angry with her. But it was Juliet's eighteenth birthday very soon. She was going to Rome.

At last, the day came. Juliet said goodbye to her parents, and then to Nurse.

'Please be happy soon, my love,' said Nurse.

'I cannot forget him,' said Juliet.

'You will,' said Nurse. 'All dreams **fade**. Soon it won't hurt any more – you'll forget.'

'Never,' said Juliet. 'I will love him always.'

She went to Rome on the next train. The city was wonderful. Everyone was perfect and very happy. At first, Juliet felt alone, but slowly she began to smile again.

One evening, she suddenly stopped walking in the street. 'I haven't thought about Romeo all day,' she remembered. She felt guilty, but that night she went out dancing.

The city of Rome was **ancient** and wonderful, and very **safe**. Juliet began to forget.

fade to go away slowly

ancient very old

safe when something bad cannot happen

31

READING CHECK

Choose the best word to complete each sentence.

a Romeo drove Tybalt's car into the *river* / *hill*.

b Juliet could not *sleep* / *run* because she was afraid.

c Juliet was *happy* / *sad* when she heard that her brother was dead.

d Romeo took a *week* / *month* to walk to Milan.

e Romeo found a job in a *factory* / *hospital* in Milan.

f For two weeks, Juliet was not free to *leave* / *go in* her house.

g Juliet *began to* / *did not begin to* forget Romeo.

h In *Rome* / *Milan*, everyone was a Perfect and was happy.

WORD WORK

Correct the underlined word in each sentence using new words from Chapter 5 in the correct form.

a The dog <u>ate</u> a large hole in the garden. ......dug......

b She often visited her dead sister's <u>house</u>. ....

c I felt <u>suspicious</u> because I did not do my homework the night before. ....

d The city of Rome is very old and it has many <u>empty</u> buildings. ....

e It's nice – and it's also important – to feel <u>guilty</u> in a large city. ....

f The bright colours of autumn will <u>forget</u> in winter. ....

g The thief wanted to hide. The mask <u>visited</u> his face. ....

h I live with my <u>police</u>, my brother, and my sister. ....

i The police were <u>suddenly</u>. They asked the thief many questions. ....

j Don't <u>cry</u>. I saw you eat my chocolates! ....

GUESS WHAT

What happens in the next chapter? Tick (✔) three boxes.

a ☐ Romeo goes to Paris.

b ☐ Nurse finds Romeo in Juliet's house.

c ☐ Romeo has not got any food.

d ☐ Romeo wins a lot of money.

e ☐ Romeo changes his face.

f ☐ Romeo stops loving Juliet.

Chapter Six ~ The Gene-fixer

In Milan, Romeo saved his money. He ate only rice and drank only water. He thought only about Juliet.

The Plague in the city was very bad. Every day there were new dead bodies in the street. A **truck** came round to get them. Soon there were two trucks, then three. The trucks took the bodies to big graves outside the city.

There was no medicine and no hope.

Romeo's flat was very cold when winter came. He shivered at night. One morning he woke up with blood on his bed. Now he had the cough, too.

gene something in your body which controls how you are or look, for example the colour of your eyes

truck a kind of big car for carrying things or people

He lost his job in the factory because he was unwell. Was this The Plague? He did not know. But it was stupid to sit and wait to die.

'I must see Juliet one more time,' Romeo thought. 'I want her to know that I still love her.'

He tried to forget the danger, and he walked back to Verona through the snow. His cough got worse.

In Verona, Romeo went in secret to Juliet's house. Carefully he went through their old gate. He remembered every stone in the wall and every tree in the garden. The flowers were all dead.

He went quietly through the garden. The house was dark – no lights were on. He climbed up the wall of the house and stared in through the window at Juliet's room. Her room was full of **dust**. She was not sleeping there any more, he could see.

Romeo wanted to cry. But just then, he heard a noise in the room.

'Who's there?' a voice said.

For a second, Romeo's heart nearly stopped with **fear**. But he knew that strange voice.

'Nurse! Is that you?' he asked.

The robot was standing in Juliet's room. It was pleased to see him. 'But Romeo, why have you come back here?' Nurse said. 'Are you mad? It is *so* dangerous.'

'I had to,' said Romeo. He coughed quietly.

'You're not well?' said Nurse. 'I'll get you some medicine.'

'Where's Juliet?' Romeo asked.

So the robot explained that Juliet was in Rome, and that her parents were still angry with her. They did not live in the house any more.

dust very small pieces of dry things in a dirty room

fear what you feel when you are afraid

'She never told them about you,' said Nurse. 'She loves you.'

'I have to see her again.'

'But that's not possible,' said the robot. 'A Normal cannot get into Rome. And you're ill. And you don't have a passport.'

'I have to go,' said Romeo.

The robot thought carefully. 'Why don't you go to a gene-fixer?' she said.

'What's a gene-fixer?' asked Romeo.

'Gene-fixers are criminals. They change your blood. They give you new eyes, new **fingerprints**. They give you a new life and a new passport. You'll need all that to get into Rome – but it's expensive and dangerous. And first you'll need some Perfect blood.'

'Does the Perfect blood have to be new, too?'

'No. The fixer only needs the genes in the blood.'

Romeo smiled thinly. He knew where he could get some Perfect blood. 'But if the gene-fixer does this to me, will I get into Rome?' he asked.

'Yes,' said the robot. 'But it's dangerous. Sometimes people die. And it's very expensive. Where will you get the money from?'

'I'll have to find a way,' said Romeo.

Romeo walked to his workshop. It was strange to be in his old home. It smelled bad and was full of dust. Blood was still on the floor, but it was dry.

He found the big green bottle. It was black with Tybalt's blood, so Romeo took it.

Outside, Romeo stood beside his brother's grave.

'I don't think that I'll visit you again here, brother,' he said.

The wind **whispered** in the trees – and when Romeo heard it, he thought of Mercutio laughing.

A visit to a gene-fixer cost 10,000 dollars. Romeo only had 1,000 dollars. 'Where am I going to find money like that?' he thought. He knew no one who was rich and could give him money.

There was one way to make big money in Verona. Every night in the city centre square, there were fights. Normals fought – men against men, women against women. And sometimes dogs fought, or chickens. The people of Verona **bet** on these fights. They won or lost a lot of money.

That evening, Romeo went to the square. Fires were burning. He could smell bad, cheap meat and blood in the **air**. He watched the first three fights but did not bet. The crowd were going wild. A fat man with a red hat was laughing and taking all their bets. Everyone was ready for the last fight. A big man from Trieste called Alberto was fighting a smaller man from Germany. The big man stood silently with his friends. He never lost fights.

The little man jumped around in the corner, alone. He was thin, and looked hungry. He also looked just like Mercutio. Romeo thought that it was a **sign**.

'How much do I win if I bet ten dollars on the little man?' asked Romeo.

'100 dollars,' said the man with the red hat.

'Good, so I bet, 1,000 dollars.'

'A thousand!' The man gave him a strange look. 'Are you sure? You'll lose your money. He's fighting Alberto. Alberto never loses.'

'I'm sure,' said Romeo. 'I won't lose.'

'You're mad!' said the man in the red hat. 'I like it. I'll take your bet.'

The fight started badly for the little man. Alberto threw him to the ground. Then he hit him hard three times.

bet to put money on a fighter, saying that he or she will win; if you are right you win money, if you are wrong you lose it

air we take this in through our mouth and nose

sign a thing that shows without words that something will or could happen

The crowd screamed and shouted. They were going wild.

The little man got up slowly. Alberto ran towards him angrily. Romeo closed his eyes.

'Please, now,' he said. 'Please help me, brother.'

The wind whispered again.

'Ooof!' There was a big noise like a tree falling.

The crowd breathed out, and then screamed even louder. When Romeo opened his eyes, the big man was lying on the ground, and the little man was standing over his body.

The man in the red hat paid Romeo 10,000 dollars.

'You're a mad fool,' he frowned. 'But you were right.'

~   ~

The next day, Romeo went to a gene-fixer. The gene-fixer was a woman with hard eyes behind her glasses. She was a doctor, but she made her money as a criminal.

'You must pay me first,' she said. 'Because if you die, you can't pay me later.'

Romeo gave her all his money. She counted it and smiled.

'Hmm. You have some Perfect blood?' she asked.

Romeo gave her the green bottle.

The gene-fixer used a knife and took a little of Tybalt's blood.

'This is good,' she said. She scanned the dry blood into her computer. 'This is good,' she said. 'It *is* Perfect blood. I'll **inject** you and change your blood and your skin. I can change your face, too, if you like.'

inject to put something into the body of a person or animal

'No,' said Romeo.

'If you don't get a new face, you'll have big trouble.'

'No! My face mustn't change.'

'Very well. The changes will fade. You have one month before you lose these new fingerprints and eyes.'

'One month is OK,' said Romeo.

'Hmm. Good. Now leave your clothes on the chair and get in that bath,' the gene-fixer told Romeo.

The bath was full of strange green water. The water was warm like tea. The gene-fixer put a mask on Romeo's face. 'You will breathe through this,' she said.

Romeo was afraid. 'I don't want to die here,' he thought.

But then he did not think any more. The gene-fixer injected him and pushed him into the water.

In seconds, Romeo was in a deep sleep. While he slept, the gene-fixer changed his blood. He got new fingerprints and new eyes. Now his eyes were blue, not brown.

Romeo dreamed of Juliet. He dreamed of seeing her again. He did not die in the bath.

When he woke up, Romeo had Tybalt's eyes, fingerprints, and blood!

READING CHECK

Match the first and second parts of these sentences.

a Romeo got ill …   1 the wind, he thought of Mercutio.

b Juliet's parents didn't live …   2 and began to cough.

c Nurse told Romeo …   3 about the gene-fixer.

d When Romeo heard the whisper of …   4 he had Tybalt's fingerprints and eyes.

e Alberto was a big, strong man …   5 who can change your blood.

f Gene-fixers are doctors …   6 and he never lost his fights.

g When Romeo woke up, …   7 in their house any more.

WORD WORK

1 Find ten more words from Chapter 6 in the green water.

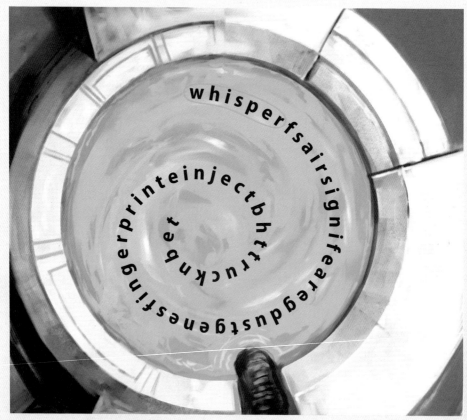

2 Complete the sentences with the words from Activity 1 in the correct form.

a Everyone's .... genes .... are different.

b In the hot wind, the .... smells of summer.

c Adam made a .... with Olly about the fight.

d The thief left a .... so the police found her.

e The snow was a .... : winter was here.

f The old house is full of ....

g Claire .... because she did not want the teacher to hear her.

h When Dave saw the large dog, he started to shake with ....

i The doctor .... me with the medicine.

j The .... is full of food for the supermarket.

GUESS WHAT

What happens in the next chapter? Tick (✔) three boxes.

a ☐ Romeo brings Juliet to Milan.

b ☐ Romeo goes to Rome.

c ☐ Juliet kisses Romeo.

d ☐ Soldiers find Romeo.

e ☐ Juliet dies.

f ☐ People think that Romeo is a Perfect.

Milan 2079

Rome 2079

Paris 2079

Chapter Seven ~ Finding Juliet

So now Romeo walked to Rome – he walked for a week. His new fingerprints and eyes were strange. They felt papery and dry. Did the gene-fixer know what she was doing?

The long walk was hard and Romeo began to cough more. He slept outside when he did not find an empty building. Luckily, because many people were dead from The Plague, a lot of houses were empty.

He saw the walls of Rome hours before he came near them. There were bright lights on them in the night, and they were very tall.

Romeo worried all the time: 'Perhaps the guards will be suspicious? Perhaps my new fingerprints and eyes won't work when they scan me? Perhaps they'll know that I am not Tybalt?'

There was only one way into Rome: through a tall gate. There were many guards and robots. The guards all had guns. They were scanning the fingerprints and eyes of everyone who went in.

Romeo shivered. He remembered when he went into the party with his brother. That was like another life. They only needed a mask and an invitation that time. This was much more difficult.

Then the wind whispered in the trees, and Romeo thought of Mercutio. Romeo felt **braver**.

'Keep calm,' he said to himself. 'You can do this.'

He walked to the gate. Everyone around him was a Perfect. They all had to wait a very long time to go into Rome. Romeo tried to breathe slowly. It was hard not to cough.

At last he was at the gate, and a guard said to him, 'Come here, please. What's your name?'

'I'm Tybalt Capulet,' said Romeo. And he thought: 'But does anyone here know that Tybalt is dead?'

'Look in here,' said the guard. He held up a bright light. Romeo knew that the light was a computer. It could look at his blood and his eyes.

brave not afraid of danger

He looked into the light. For a long time nothing happened. Romeo could hear his heart. His mouth was dry.

At last the guard said, 'Very good. Put your finger in here.'

Romeo put his finger inside a white box. The computer inside the box scanned his fingerprint.

'Please,' thought Romeo. 'Please work.'

'OK,' the guard said at last. 'Welcome to Rome, Mr Capulet.'

Romeo went through the gate. He wanted to smile but he could not enjoy himself yet. 'First I must find Juliet... oh, Juliet', he thought.

The ancient city of Rome was like another world. There was no dust or dying trees. Everything was **clean**. Everyone was beautiful – and nobody was ill.

But the streets were too tidy. It did not look real.

This was not the strangest thing. 'I've never seen so many happy people,' Romeo thought. There were no frowns on people's faces. No one was angry. No one was coughing blood. No one looked thin or tired. Everyone was calm. 'These people don't fight for food,' Romeo thought. He could not stop staring. He began to feel angry. It was not right: the Perfects had all this, and Normal people had nothing.

clean not dirty

Then Romeo coughed. Luckily the cough was quiet, but three people looked at him. He hid his face and turned away before they asked any questions.

He remembered that he must find Juliet fast.

'Excuse me,' he asked a man. 'How do I find someone in Rome?'

'What is their name?' smiled the man. 'Perhaps I know them.'

Romeo was worried. He could not tell anyone his secret. 'I'm looking for a girl called Juliet Capulet.'

'Oh, her!' said the man. 'Yes! I know her. Everyone knows her. She's very beautiful.'

'She is...', said Romeo. But he felt uncomfortable. 'Why does everyone know her?'

'She **acts** in the theatre. She's very good, but when you watch her, you know that she has a broken heart. That's unusual in Rome. I think that's why people like her.'

'How do I get to the theatre?' asked Romeo.

'You're lucky!' said the man. 'I'm going there now. A **show**'s starting in a few minutes and I think that Juliet Capulet's in it. Will you come with me?'

Romeo agreed. He was very worried now.

The theatre was in the centre of Rome. It was ancient. The seats were stone stairs in a ring around the **stage**.

Romeo sat next to the man. His name was Lorenzo. He talked a lot, but Romeo said nothing. He was trying hard not to cough.

There were lots of people in the theatre – they were all Perfects, of course. The show started. It was a story about a

act to speak and move in a play or film

show a play with people acting at the theatre, or something you watch on TV

stage where people stand when they act a play or do a show

44

soldier who was brave but stupid. The soldier did not know that his best friend wanted to kill him and take his wife.

Juliet was acting as the soldier's wife.

When she came onto the stage, Romeo wanted to shout out. He was so happy to see her. She was even more beautiful than before. He stared at her and forgot everything. Everyone in the theatre did the same. They watched only her. She acted so well. She was wonderful, and everything felt real when she spoke.

It was a long time before Romeo remembered his plan. At last, he began to think. He needed to speak to her.

'I'll find her when the show finishes,' he thought. 'And I'll tell her...'

He stopped. He did not know what to say. His words sounded stupid.

'How can I ask her to come with me?' he thought. 'Hello Juliet! Please leave this happy place, because I cannot stay here. Please come with me to my world. There, everyone is dying of The Plague, and everything is filthy and broken. Please leave all your friends, and your wonderful life here. Please leave with me, *for* me. Oh and... I am dying.'

Romeo loved Juliet so much, but suddenly he knew that he would never see her again.

'I'll leave at once,' he decided. 'I'll watch the show, and then I'll go. I won't speak to her. She's too happy here.'

The story in the show was very good. The soldier's best friend lied about everything. Because of his lies, the brave but stupid soldier was suspicious of his wife. In the end, the soldier got very angry and killed his wife.

Romeo watched when Juliet died in the show. He began to cry. All the other people in the theatre were crying, too. For a few minutes, Romeo forgot everything. He coughed. A little blood fell on his hand.

Lorenzo, sitting next to him, began shouting.

'The Plague! The Plague! This man has The Plague! He's coughing blood!'

Then everyone in the theatre began shouting. 'He's a **terrorist**!'

The show on the stage stopped. The crowd began to move away from Romeo. Everyone was pushing to get away from him. They did not want to get The Plague.

Romeo wanted to run, but he knew that he would not get far.

'I'm Romeo!' he shouted. 'Romeo!'

On the stage, Juliet turned white. She was looking up at him.

'I love you!' shouted Romeo. He coughed again and the people screamed.

'He's got The Plague. Terrorist!'

Lots of soldiers were coming through the crowd.

'Get down!' they shouted. 'Don't move. Put your hands above your head!'

terrorist a person who does violent things to get change

Romeo was staring at Juliet. He knew that he would never see her again. He smiled.

'Goodbye,' he said.

Juliet was still staring at him. She could not move.

'She'll know that I tried,' Romeo thought. 'And she'll have a long and happy life.'

The soldiers came to Romeo. They were wearing masks over their mouths.

'Who are you?' one of them shouted.

Romeo coughed, and the soldiers were afraid. 'Don't cough! Get down or we'll shoot you.'

They moved their guns. Romeo sat in his seat.

'What's your name?' one of them asked again.

'My name's Romeo. You can take me now.'

The soldiers took him away. Romeo did not look back.

READING CHECK

Match the sentences with the people.

Romeo

Juliet

a … has to get past the guards in Rome.

b … has never been to Rome.

c … is acting in a show at the theatre.

d … is famous.

e … sits in the theatre with all the Perfects.

f … coughs and blood comes out of his mouth.

g … acts on the stage as a soldier's wife.

h … dies in the show and makes everyone in the theatre cry.

i … has to go with the soldiers.

WORD WORK

1 Find five more words from Chapter 7 in the letter square.

act   brave   clean   ~~show~~   stage   terrorist

B	C	D	A	S	A	C	T	Z
V	L	N	N	H	A	W	L	S
T	E	R	R	O	R	I	S	T
A	A	Q	P	W	M	R	B	A
X	N	T	B	Y	F	J	K	G
Z	E	U	E	B	R	A	V	E

2 Complete the sentences with the words from Activity 1 in the correct form.

a Do you have any tickets for the new .....show.....?

b When he saw the big bear, Claude did not feel very ....

c I know that man. He .... in that new film.

d The .... carried a gun and wore a mask.

e Shakespeare wrote 'All the world's a .... '.

f My car's very .... now! It was very dirty.

GUESS WHAT

What happens in the next chapter? Tick (✔) three boxes.

a ☐ Romeo is in prison.

b ☐ Juliet saves Romeo from prison.

c ☐ Romeo dies.

d ☐ Romeo and Juliet escape together.

e ☐ Nurse saves Romeo and Juliet.

f ☐ Juliet dies.

The Colosseum in Rome today.

Chapter Eight ~ Romeo and Juliet

The guards took Romeo into a prison. From the outside the building looked ancient, but inside it was modern, white and clean. They put Romeo in a room with a bed, a chair, and no windows. They locked the door. Romeo closed his eyes and remembered Juliet. She looked so beautiful on the stage. But he was **sad** – and suspicious: 'Why didn't she say anything?' he thought. 'Why didn't she say my name?'

Then Romeo thought of something more terrible: perhaps she didn't love him any more? She had a new life here in Rome. 'Perhaps she has forgotten me?' he thought.

After that, Romeo wanted to die. He could not forget his fears. He sat all alone in the clean, white room.

'If the soldiers shoot me here, I'll die quickly,' he thought.

After a long time, the door opened softly. A man in a white coat came in. He was wearing a mask. 'I'm Dr Angelo,' he said. 'If you tell me how you got into Rome, I can help you.'

'How will you help me?' said Romeo. 'Will you free me?'

'I cannot do that,' said the doctor. 'You've broken the **law**. You won't leave this prison. But I can get you food and water.'

'Just kill me quickly,' said Romeo. 'I don't want your help.'

'Why did you come to Rome?' asked the doctor. 'Who sent you? Tell me!'

'No one,' said Romeo.

'Were you trying to give The Coughing Plague to Perfects?' said the doctor. 'Are you a terrorist?'

'No,' said Romeo. 'I'm just a fool.'

'Then why did you come here?'

Romeo did not want to get Juliet into trouble. He said nothing. The doctor frowned. 'I can't help you if you don't help me.'

'Then kill me.' said Romeo. 'I'm ready to die.'

The doctor frowned again and left the room. Two soldiers came in. They did not kill Romeo. They **tied** him to the bed

sad not happy

law the rules that say what people must or must not do

tie to keep something in place with string or rope

and injected him with medicine. The medicine helped with The Plague, and Romeo's cough stopped. The soldiers also gave Romeo food and water. Three days later, Dr Angelo came again to the prison.

'Why are you keeping me alive?' Romeo asked him.

'So we can learn,' said the doctor. 'We want to know how you changed your body. Who did this? Who gave you Perfect blood?'

Romeo did not want to help the Perfects. He said nothing.

'If we want you to talk, you will talk,' said Dr Angelo.

'How?' asked Romeo.

'Everyone talks in the end,' said the doctor. 'Even terrorists, like you.'

'You're giving me food and medicine, and making me better because you want to **torture** me?' asked Romeo. 'You Perfects are **monsters**.'

'We need to know,' said Dr Angelo. 'I will come again in the morning. If you do not talk then, we'll stop being nice. It will not go well for you. I think that you'll talk to me tomorrow, yes?'

Romeo did not like Dr Angelo. He did not like his calm voice, and his little smile. 'What can I do? How can I escape?' Romeo thought that night. 'They have really **trapped** me.'

Romeo could not sleep. In the morning, his door opened.

'Go away!' he shouted. 'I won't tell you anything.'

'Be quiet, you filthy Normal!' said a hard voice. It was a woman's voice, and Romeo did not know it. She spoke to the guards outside. 'I'm taking this terrorist away – we're going to question him.'

'Very good,' said a guard. 'What happened to Dr Angelo?'

'He's feeling ill this morning, so I'm here,' the woman said.

'Do you need me to come with you?' asked the guard.

'No, I don't,' the woman replied coldly. Romeo already **hated** this woman more than Dr Angelo. 'Put the mask on his face,' she told the guard. 'I don't want to look at him and I don't want to get The Plague.'

torture to hurt somebody because you want to learn things from them, or be unkind to them

monster someone or something that does very bad things

trap to catch somebody and stop them leaving somewhere

hate not to like

51

The bed had wheels, and with Romeo on it, the woman began to push the bed out through the door. She walked quickly.

Romeo could not see anything, but he heard the woman when she talked to the guards.

'I hate terrorists,' she said. 'We're going to hurt him a lot.'

The guards laughed.

Then the bed was moving out into the street. The birds were singing in the trees. Romeo breathed the clean air.

'Where are you taking me?' he asked.

'Shut up, Normal!' the woman shouted.

'You tell him!' said a guard.

'Oh, I will,' said the woman.

She pushed Romeo along a small road. Now she was hurrying. The sounds of the city were quieter. Suddenly, Romeo heard water. Was it a river?

'What's happening?' he shouted.

'Be quiet, you fool!' the woman whispered – but her voice was different now. Then she pulled off his mask and kissed him.

'Juliet!' said Romeo, when the wonderful kiss stopped at last. He looked at her beautiful face. 'You came for me!'

Juliet held him in her arms. 'Of course! I love you so much.'

Romeo remembered everything: her eyes, her nose, her soft hair. He felt her wet face – she was crying and laughing, all at once.

He was so happy – he thought that his heart was going to stop.

'What have they done to you, Romeo?' Juliet asked.

'Nothing. I'm fine.'

'You're so brave!' said Juliet. 'I love you so much!'

'Not as brave as you,' said Romeo. 'You're great at acting. I hated that doctor woman!'

'Thank you,' said Juliet. 'I enjoyed that. Now, how do I get you out of this bed? We need to go.'

Suddenly Romeo felt sad. 'No,' he thought. What was he doing?

'Leave me here,' he said.

'What are you talking about?' Juliet was angry. 'Do you know how dangerous this is? They'll start looking for us soon.'

'But we can't be together,' said Romeo. 'If you leave Rome, you'll leave all this behind. You won't act on the stage any more.'

'You fool! I love you! I cannot live without you, Romeo,' said Juliet. 'I have a small boat over there on the river. It will take us out of the city.'

'But if you leave Rome, you'll get ill.'

'It doesn't matter!'

'I'm dying, Juliet. I have The Plague,' Romeo told her.

'I have money,' said Juliet. 'We'll go to Paris. We'll find medicine. It's what we planned...'

'But...'

'No! We'll be happy together or we'll die together.'

Romeo could not fight any more. He did not want to.

'Let's go then!' he said.

Juliet's boat was waiting on the river. They climbed inside and moved silently out onto the water. Up ahead, the great walls of Rome stood across the river. But their boat was small and easily went through a hole in the water-gate.

'We're free!' said Juliet.

They both laughed. Romeo laughed hard, and he began to cough. Blood fell on the bottom of the boat.

'I'm so sorry about your brother,' said Juliet.

'I'm so sorry about Tybalt,' said Romeo.

'Don't be,' Juliet told him. She gave a little cough.

The wind whispered in the trees and they both thought of Mercutio.

ACTIVITIES

READING CHECK

Put these sentences in the correct order. Number them 1–8.

a ☐ A woman takes Romeo out of the prison.

b ☐ Dr Angelo talks to Romeo.

c ☐ Romeo laughs in the boat, and then he coughs.

d ☐ The woman is Juliet. She kisses Romeo.

e ☐ The guards take Romeo into a prison.

f ☐ Juliet gives a little cough.

g ☐ Two soldiers tie Romeo to a bed.

h ☐ Romeo and Juliet get in a boat on the river and leave Rome.

WORD WORK

1 Use the words in the box in the correct form to complete Juliet's diary.

| brave   hate   law   monster   sad   tie   torture   trap |

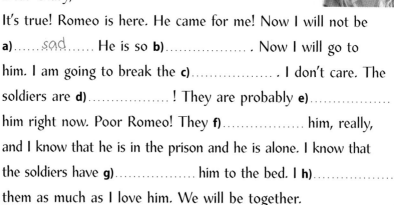

May 25th

Dear Diary,

It's true! Romeo is here. He came for me! Now I will not be
a) ......sad...... He is so **b)** .... Now I will go to
him. I am going to break the **c)** .... I don't care. The
soldiers are **d)** .... ! They are probably **e)** ....
him right now. Poor Romeo! They **f)** .... him, really,
and I know that he is in the prison and he is alone. I know that
the soldiers have **g)** .... him to the bed. I **h)** ....
them as much as I love him. We will be together.

54

2 Find words from Chapter 8 in the word puzzle to match the definitions.

s	a	e
to	i	d
l	a	er
t	rtu	ap
mo	nst	w
t	r	e
h	at	re

a ...... sad .... Not happy.

b .... Something that tells you what you must or must not do.

c .... To hurt somebody because you want to make them feel bad, or to be unkind to them.

d .... To keep something in place with a rope.

e .... To catch somebody and stop them leaving somewhere.

f .... A terrible person.

g .... Not to like.

GUESS WHAT

What do you think happens after the story ends? Choose from these ideas, or add your own.

a ☐ Romeo and Juliet both die of The Plague.

b ☐ Romeo and Juliet find medicine and live in Paris.

c ☐ Juliet's parents hunt them and find them.

d ☐ The Normals fight against the Perfects and win.

e ☐ ....

f ☐ ....

PROJECT A *The End of the World*

1 Shakespeare wrote his famous play *Romeo and Juliet* in about 1597. This story of Romeo and Juliet happens in the year 2079. Think about how the world could change or end in a hundred years! Match the pictures with the sentences on page 57.

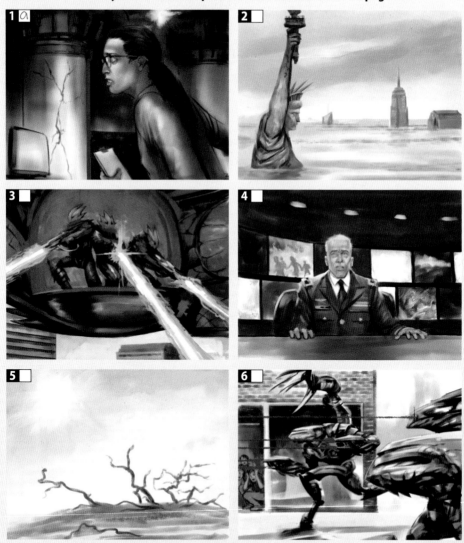

a A mad doctor makes a terrible plague and many people die. ....

b The countries of the world build robots that fight each other. People hide. ....

c Clever computers begin to hunt people. Soldiers can't help. ....

d Monsters arrive from another world with large guns. ....

e The world gets too hot. Plants can't grow and there is no water. ....

f Water covers the world. People leave. They need to find a safe world. ....

2 **Look at the notes about how the world could change. Then complete the report.**

How did it start?	Angry people start to fight.
What happens?	Soon each country of the world is fighting, it isn't safe.
What did you do?	Find a clever computer, build a special machine.
Where did you go?	Fly to a different world, there is no fighting there.
What did you do next?	Go back to find my family and friends, help other people to escape.

It all starts when people are **a)** .... so they start to **b)** ....

Soon each country of the world is fighting. It isn't **c)** .... anywhere. So I find a

d) .... computer and **e)** .... a special machine. I fly to a different

f) .... where there is **g)** .... fighting. Then I go back to find my

h) .... and friends. I help other people to **i)** ...., too.

3 **Choose a different way the world could change. Write some notes using the table below. Then write a short report using your notes.**

How did it start?	
What happens?	
What did you do?	
Where did you go?	
What did you do next?	

PROJECT B   *Character backstories*

A backstory tells what happened to a character before the story begins. We understand a character better if we know their backstory.

1 Match each backstory with a character from *Romeo and Juliet 2079*.

a When he was a boy, his mother and father died from The
Coughing Plague. He lived on the streets and was always
hungry. One day, he saw a fight in the square in the city
centre. The people of Verona bet on these fights. He met a
fat man with a red hat. He fought for the man and won lots
of money. After that, he decided to fight every day and he
never loses. ☐

b He was the youngest son. When he and his brother were
little, his father told them stories: in the old times, there were
no Perfects or Normals, his father said. He wanted to read
and write, but his parents had no money so he could not go
to school. He loved dreaming, and talking – much more than
he liked working. His father and mother died young. ☐

c She was made in a special workshop. Mr Capulet bought her
for a lot of money and took her to his house. Then she met
Mrs Capulet and her children. Now she lives with them. She
is a teacher. She is also a guard. When she met Juliet, she
made her first friend. ☐

d She was born in Verona. She has an older brother. Her mother
and father are very rich and enjoy spending money on large
parties. She likes reading and one day she wants to be an
actress. She has a nurse who is a robot. She has never been
to the Normals' city. She has to go to Rome when she is
eighteen. ☐

PROJECTS

2 Read these backstory sentences. Who do they belong to? Mark them R (Romeo) or T (Tybalt).

a He never went to school but he was clever with his hands.

b He could drive a car – badly, but he could not mend one.

c His father was rich and lived in a large house.

d His father was very poor and died young.

e Before he was born, doctors had made him perfect.

f His mother died when his brother was still a young boy.

g He liked wearing beautiful clothes and having expensive parties.

h He liked mending things.

3 Complete the gene-fixer's backstory with the words in the box.

| angry | bath | blood | fingerprints | Normal | parents | Plague | rich | Rome | school |

I was born a Perfect, and I lived in a large house in Verona with my **a)** . . . . I went to **b)** . . . . and then learned to be a doctor. My family had money, but we were not as **c)** . . . . as many other Perfects. My parents wanted to move to **d)** . . . . , but we did not have enough money. Then they caught The Coughing **e)** . . . . in Verona and they died. I was very **f)** . . . .

A few months later, I was working for a very important doctor. One day, he wanted to show me something very special. He could change a Normal's **g)** . . . . so they looked like a Perfect. He could make new eyes and **h)** . . . . , too. 'Why are you telling me this?' I asked. 'Because my wife and I want to go to Rome,' the doctor said. 'The Coughing Plague is not there. But she is a **i)** . . . . Will you help us?' I agreed to help him.

When he and his wife left, I then had the doctor's computer and a **j)** . . . . of strange green water. 'Normals will pay 10,000 dollars to become Perfects. Now I can make some money and I will be rich!' I thought.

4 Complete the backstory about Romeo's father with the words from the box.

clothes	cough	gardens	Mercutio	money	old
Perfect	robot	Romeo	The Plague	Verona	wife

I was born in **a)** . . . . When I was a boy, everyone was born the same. People

weren't Normal or **b)** . . . . Everyone went to school and had **c)** . . . . ,

and a car. Everyone lived until they were **d)** . . . . I met my **e)** . . . .

when I worked for a Perfect in their **f)** . . . . She worked at the Perfect's house, too,

mending **g)** . . . . , and looking after the children because the rich family did not

have a **h)** . . . . But then **i)** . . . . was born, and a few years later

j) . . . . arrived. One day, my wife had a bad **k)** . . . . , and then I began

to cough, too. We both had **l)** . . . .

5 Imagine the backstories of Tybalt's friend Sampson or one of the guards working in Rome. Look at the questions and write notes.

Sampson

When and where were you born?
How did you meet Tybalt?
Do you like him?
What do you want to do when you are older?

The guard

When and where were you born?
How did you become a guard?
Do you like being a guard?
What do you want to do next?

6 Now write a backstory for Sampson or the guard.

GRAMMAR CHECK

Adverbs

We use some adverbs to talk about *how* something is done.

Romeo ran away quickly.   *'What are you doing?' he asked nicely.*

We make adverbs from adjectives by adding -ly.

nice – nicely   *strange – strangely*

For adjectives that end in -y we change -y to -i and add -ly.

lazy – lazily   *heavy – heavily*

Some adverbs are irregular. You will have to learn these forms.

good – well

1 Complete the sentences. Make an adverb from the best adjective in brackets.

a Mercutio worked ..... *lazily* ..... because he liked talking much more than working.
(*lazy / good*)

b Mercutio and Romeo looked at each other .... in Romeo's workshop.
(*cold / nice*)

c Romeo walked .... away from the party into the garden. (*quick / slow*)

d Mercutio and Romeo went .... though the garden
gate. (*thin / quiet*)

e Romeo and Juliet met .... every day for a
month. (*secret / soft*)

f People said that in Paris, Normals and Perfects lived
together .... (*happy / sad*)

g After Tybalt hurt Mercutio, Romeo ran
.... to Tybalt. (*loving / angry*)

h Juliet acted .... and soon she was very
famous. (*good / bad*)

i Romeo and Juliet's boat was small and
.... went through a hole in the water-
gate. (*bad / easy*)

GRAMMAR CHECK

Present Perfect and Past Simple

We use the Present Perfect to talk about things happening at some time in the past without saying when.

Have you been to Verona? Yes, I have.   I've seen a photograph of Juliet. But I haven't met her.

We can also use it for things that happened in the past and continue in the present.

I've known Romeo for fifteen years. (for + a period of time)

We use the Past Simple for finished past actions. Many Past Simple verbs end in -d (arrived), -ed (helped), or -ied (tried). There are also many irregular verbs.

met – I met Juliet two days ago.

2 **Complete this email from Juliet to Nurse in the Present Perfect or the Past Simple using the words from the box.**

did	didn't like	found	has been	has built	has coughed	has fallen	~~have been~~
have begun	have never been	said	stopped	walked	went		

Dear Nurse,

Romeo and I **a)** ...have been... (be) in Paris for three weeks now. At first, we
b) .... (not like) the city because the people were not very friendly.
We **c)** .... (find) jobs. I **d)** .... (begin) working as an actress
in a little theatre. Romeo is working at the theatre, too. He **e)** .... (build)
wonderful things. Now we have got enough money for medicine. Romeo
f) .... (cough) for six months, but yesterday he **g)** .... (stop)
at last.
Last night, we **h)** .... (go) out to dinner to celebrate. We **i)** ....
(walk) to the river. Did you know that the old bridge **j)** .... (fall) down?
Someone **k)** .... (say) that terrorists **l)** .... (do) it. They say that
the bridge **m)** .... (be) broken for two years.

I **n)** .... (never be) so happy.

Love, Juliet

GRAMMAR CHECK

Past Simple information questions

We use question words (how, who, what, why, when, and where) in information questions. We answer these questions with information. In Past Simple questions, most verbs take did + subject + infinitive without *to*.

How did Tybalt crash his car into a tree? He was being stupid.

Why did Tybalt scream? Because Mercutio put hot tea in his eyes.

With the verb be, we put the subject after the verb to make Past Simple questions.

Who was Alberto? He was a big fighter.

3 Complete each question with a question word from the box. Match the answers below with the questions.

| what   who   how   ~~why~~   who   how   why   where |

a ......Why...... was Tybalt's car in the workshop? ☒ 8

b .... did Romeo and Mercutio get into the party at Juliet's house? ☐

c .... did they wear masks to the party? ☐

d .... did Tybalt see at the party? ☐

e .... did Romeo and Juliet meet? ☐

f .... was the gene-fixer? ☐

g .... did Romeo get into Rome? ☐

h .... were Tybalt's eyes like? ☐

1 She was a doctor, but money had made her a criminal.

2 They found Tybalt's invitation and wore masks.

3 Because they wanted to hide from Tybalt.

4 He went to the gene-fixer and got new eyes and fingerprints.

5 They met in the garden.

6 He saw Mercutio at the party.

7 His eyes were blue.

8 Because he had crashed it into a tree.

GRAMMAR CHECK

Linkers: *so* and *because*

We use so to link two sentences when the second sentence explains a result.

Romeo coughed at the theatre <u>so the soldiers came with guns.</u>

(= result of first part of sentence)

We use because to link two sentences when the second sentence explains a reason.

No Normals could go into Rome <u>because the people were afraid of The Coughing Plague.</u>

(= reason for first part of sentence)

4 Complete the sentences using *so* or *because*.

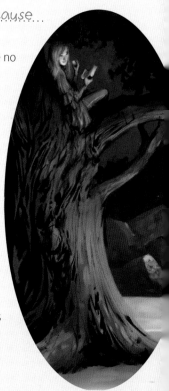

a Perfects thought that they were better than Normals ...*because*... before they were born, doctors changed them.

b Romeo had no money in Verona .... there were no cars to mend.

c Tybalt did not want his father to know about his car accident .... he asked Romeo to mend his car.

d Juliet was hiding up the tree .... she didn't like the party.

e Tybalt was not watching Mercutio .... he was surprised when Mercutio hit him on the head.

f Romeo walked to Rome .... he could see Juliet again.

g Romeo lost his job in the factory in Milan .... he was unwell.

h Romeo couldn't lie to Juliet .... he ran away.

i Romeo bought a gun .... there were dangerous people in the mountains.

GRAMMAR

GRAMMAR CHECK

Participle clauses

Sometimes we talk about two actions that happen at the same time.

Romeo was eating at the table. He read a book.

We can use a participle clause to link the two actions more closely. To do this we use the -ing form of the verb and put a comma in front of the participle clause.

Romeo was eating at the table, reading a book.

5 Write the sentences again as one sentence with a participle clause.

a Juliet went to the Normals' city. She hid her face.
Juliet went to the Normals' city, hiding her face.

b Nurse went into Juliet's empty room. She thought about Juliet.
....

c Romeo took the gun in his hand. He felt afraid.
....

d Mercutio danced wildly. He was smiling and moving his arms.
....

e 'I'm not working,' said Mercutio. He put his hands in his pockets.
....

f Romeo ate only rice. He wanted to save his money.
....

g Tybalt bought another car. He spent all of his money.
....

h 'Get down,' shouted the soldiers. They pushed the crowd.
....

i Juliet talked and Romeo watched. He was thinking about Paris.
....

j 'I hate you,' screamed Tybalt. He broke down the workshop door.
....

GRAMMAR CHECK

Time clauses with *before*, *after*, and *when*

Before links a later action with an earlier main action.

Before the sun was up, <u>Romeo ran into the hills.</u>

                               (= earlier action)

After links an earlier action with a later action.

<u>*Juliet went secretly to Romeo's workshop*</u> *after two weeks in her room.*

(= later action)

When links two actions near in time.

Mercutio hit Tybalt when Tybalt pointed his gun at Romeo.

When we write the time clause first, we use a comma.

When he woke up, Romeo had Tybalt's eyes.

6 Complete the sentences with *before*, *after*, or *when*.

a ......When...... Mercutio and Romeo were young, their father told them stories.

b People saw the gates of Rome hours .... they came near to them.

c Juliet was waiting at the garden gate .... Romeo arrived.

d Romeo had one month .... he lost his new fingerprints and eyes.

e .... a long time, the prison door opened slowly.

f Romeo saw Tybalt's car outside .... he arrived at the workshop.

g Romeo hid his face .... the guards could ask him any questions.

7 Match the sentences about Juliet.

a When her parents had a party,   **1** Juliet went to help him

b She could see Romeo's face after   **2** she hid up a tree

c Before Juliet met Romeo,   **3** he took off his mask

d ... when she was eighteen.   **4** she had never been to the Normals' city

e After Romeo was taken by the guards,   **5** Juliet had to go to Rome